C000217375

*Dedicated to my spectacular sister,
the playwright Helen K Parker.
Always with us.*

Cormorant

Elizabeth Parker

Seren is the book imprint of
Poetry Wales Press Ltd.
Suite 6, 4 Derwen Road, Bridgend,
Wales, CF31 1LH

www.serenbooks.com
Follow us on social media @SerenBooks

The right of Elizabeth Parker to be identified as
the author of this work has been asserted in accordance
with the Copyright, Designs and Patents Act, 1988.

© Elizabeth Parker, 2024.

ISBN: 978-1-78172-736-2
ebook: 978-1-78172-737-9

A CIP record for this title is available from the British Library.

All rights reserved. No part of this publication may be reproduced,
stored in a retrieval system, or transmitted at any time or by any means,
electronic, mechanical, photocopying, recording or otherwise without
the prior permission of the copyright holder.

The publisher acknowledges the financial assistance of the Books Council of Wales.

Cover painting: *10,000 Steps* by Gemma Compton.

Printed in Bembo by 4edge Limited, Essex.

Contents

Today
perched cormorant
please do not preen my gaze
from your wing. Let me stay a while.

Cormorant

on rivers
black curl from the Avon.

Cormorant at source
plucking at tributaries
where elvers string their bodies
to the current.

Cormorant at confluence
of salt and fresh, deep and shallow
rivers changing names.

Cormorant at mouth
streak above the estuary
brandishing fish.

Sea Cormorant
dipping feet to land
ripping the Atlantic.

Cormorant beyond
hinterlands, borderlands
backwaters.

Cormorant holding fast
as swallows, sand martins
flee winter.

Cormorant inland
locked to reservoirs, urban rivers
when I can't think past this city.

Cormorant in colonies
six omens in a dying beech.

Slow city cormorant
wings half-spread on a jetty
hooked on air to dry.

Cormorant grand
landing full-stretched
wake of shredded water

the harbour's centrepiece
dark as cast iron.

I want cormorant every day
nothing in my life so streamlined
as the sleek hook.

Black crucifix
surfacing from its dive,
spirit of the drowned.

Greville Smyth Park

In Three Shades

These moments light a dull month.
Winter sun makes bullion

of apartments across the park.
We thought the dark had set in

until this morning: our grief
beaten into glancing gold.

–

Late afternoon re-defines,
light keeping to clearer lines.

The sky a promise: grey glare
above the fields, boundary

dotted by a football game,
shadows against the dun haze

of trees, apartments; no pall,
but stark with stored light

above white shirts, calls – *Man on!* –
school jumpers strewn for goals.

–

Evening's bitten path – autumn
chewed to mush by paws, shoes, bike treads –

leads us further from the glow.
That maple on Rownham Close

has dropped its blaze, our losses
measured in the fall – colour

mashed to mud. All melds, all blends
in paths mired with hopeful plans,

disappointments glimpsed in the mulch.
Failures, husks of mischance

sink, with us, into the hush;
dusk's thickening forgiveness.

Coulouvray

It has begun when we arrive:
the darkening you described.

You've never brought a woman here:
your father's stone cottage, the ruin next door.

I came to gather sun in my skin
but the day blackens fast,
trees to obelisks.

I miss my city dark
thinned by street lamps.

This darkness inks me in,
blots sloped pastures,
a bull behind a fence.

It can't be mapped:
my hands, my footing unsure.

Here, my fingers slip.
Here, it brushes me with insect shells,
brittle wings.

In places it is sharp.
Its edges must be learnt.

Give me grey or weaker black
not this heft of pitch
rubbled with wrecked cottages
storing thickly, gaping for more.

Garlic

I have been thinking too far.
For now, rejoice in these tooths of garlic.

Let a memory fall
to melt in the pan:

his fingers slipping paper from
a clove, passing it to me.

I waited for the next. 'Just
use the one. We don't want to overpower.'

Everything tasted different then.
These days, I savour myself.

Coriander by the fistful.
Sloshes of red wine.
Butter.
Blizzards of garlic.

Waiting For The Cormorant

Cannop Ponds, 2019

We skim the southern lake:
deckchairs on the verge of the gravel road,
a portable TV, picnic site rootled by boar,
queue at the 'Green Tomato' coffee hut.

Through the kissing gate, into the hush
of the northern lake. He is on a jetty,
waiting for the cormorant.

We tell him: 'Its roost is the southern lake —
the same crooked stick over the water.'
Yet he stays put.
'You could be here for hours.
We've never seen it here', we say.

Road barely heard up a high bank
rugged with fern, rocks, birch.

Lakeside oaks
leaning and fallen.

Drone of the Stoneworks
from the far bank.

That evening,
I hear his reasons:

I want it framed by quiet

half-sunk boughs

reed beds

the hum that reassures
we're far from road and drill

a row of sleeping mallard.

You Began

For my sons Jack and Danny

I

You began with the first slab of the Slighe Chualann,
ancient road reeling from the eyes of the High King.
At the seat of Tara, you began.

You began with forgotten warriors
their battles leached to bedrock.

You began with Cu Cuchulain.

Under the Standing Stone, you began.

In Armagh, in Derry;
in Fermanagh, in Tyrone, in Cavan,
on bloodied borders, you began.

You began with your sin-sin-seanmháthair
at Dublin Port, in the mouth of the Liffey, you began.

II

You began on the Irish Sea,
on the deck of the steam packet:
your sin-sin-seanmháthair
watching Ireland shrink.

You began beside the Mersey
on the Albert Dock.
In the sea-breath of migrants, you began.

III

You began with your sin-seanathair
cleaning the windows of Littlewoods.
In the folds of a chamois cloth, you began.

You began in a Bootle terrace,
your great-nanny folding over,
re-hemming.

You began with the click of bobbins,
in the eye of a Singer needle
dipping to offcuts,
making new from second-hand.

You began in dustings of flour.
You began in the council house
where she baked every day:
apple pies, scones, currant flats.

You began in the Blitz,
the munitions factory
where her quick fingers
cased bullets, stuffed shells.

In the yellow cast of cordite, you began.

IV

You began in The Midlands
in the eyes of master craftsmen
reading the grain.

You began with tap of hammer on chisel,
slices furling over the bevelled bite.
You began in nick and groove,
in mortise and chamfer,
in the fine-tuned fingers of artisans.

You began in Smethwick,
in the moulds of pattern-makers
casting in wood and wax.

V

You began in The Forest Of Dean,
in Cannop Valley; around your beginning,
sap shuttled through spruce, fir, pine
to pinnacles circled by buzzards.

You began in the rise of giants
healing their wounds with glisters of resin.
You began in its sweet, sticky grasp,
in kernels cherishing
trapped insects.

VI

You began in Bristol, beside the Avon;
in drifts of algae, flotsam thronging
the walls of the floating harbour,
the cormorant drying its wings on a buoy,
black prow of SS Great Britain,
the harbourmaster's churning wake.

VII

You began in summer,
at the foot of Pen y Fan.

I gave up after the first slope,
left your father to summit.

Sun was silvering the mud
as I passed my former, heavy steps –
deep cut of my treads
leading back to a stream
threading brown rocks
near the car park gate.
In rills of freshwater, you began.

Royal Fort Gardens

Before he said it, she was coalescing
with late sun. Together,
they perused sloped lawns,
took their time with honeysuckle,
the yew tree pronouncing
its impenetrability.

His words are in the garden.

Allium buds are splitting.
Aphids suck the pink rambler rose;
leaves decked in their white shells.
He's near the willow arch, blurred.
She's picking through sharp grasses.

His words are in the garden.

She was tall.
Sheened arms to stirred canopy.
She was serene:
draped her gaze amidst the white tatters
of the handkerchief tree.

His words are in the garden.

She is keeping to the shade
of the black mulberry,
head bowed over chaff and gnats,
scrammed ankles.

Paddy's Ashes

For my grandfather John Patrick Riley

As she tipped you into the four winds
from the top of Sliabh Foy,
Marie recited Yeats'
'To A Child Dancing In The Wind':
Dance there upon the shore.

Your favourite poem –
I learn, decades later, on the phone –
spoken as you were poured
into the four winds
'one crisp morning'
'one very frosty morning.'

'You could see north, south, east, west,
Dundalk and Nury.
A TV mast marks the point
near Long Woman's Grave.'

'It was February.
The ground was hard underfoot.
The grass was crunching.
So clear. No haze.
You could see forever.

Someone was cutting peat
with a long, narrow shovel.
A stack of turf. Sods of bog
let to dry out, then burnt.
Poor man's coal.'

Why didn't I ask before?
Decades later, learning
how you were poured
into the four winds
at the top of Sliabh Foy

near Long Woman's Grave,
near someone cutting,
stacking turf
to burn.
What need have you to dread
The monstrous crying of wind!

Next Stop Lockdown

Bristol, February 2020

People on the bus
are frail and surprised,
their eyes shoal to every movement.

Someone has left her scent in my seat.
It is almost the fragrance
I can no longer afford, its tint
overlaying stiff moquette
overlaying the stale.

They are frail, surprised,
hold their bags close.

A can of beer falls
from a young man's rucksack,
rolls under the seats.

A man sneezes. A lady tuts.
He sneezes again, doesn't raise a hand.
She mutters 'use a hankie'

while the woman beside me lets her eyes close,

is jolted awake
by a girl narking with the driver,
holding the straphanger,
scowling down the aisle.

10,000 Steps

After Gemma Compton's painting '10,000 Steps' (cover image), painted in Lockdown

We walked to the harbour every day.
From clamour of paintings, objects. From her wrecked body
that can't be silenced, cries of fractured spine, to Avon,
broadening,
until she is the light

slicking mudbanks, her breath the breeze
lifting alder's catkins, green spheres of London Plane;
her breath the current, seeming slow, seeming to ease
dun green Avon.

My trainers got wrecked.
We saw a cormorant every day.
You know, that tree. On Coronation Road.
By the bridge.

She dips the tip;
conjures, with sleight of brush,
the flash on black neck.
Flicks, brisk strokes
for light striking feather filaments,

for prism of pigments,
air pockets blocking, absorbing wavelengths,
flinging back turquoise – all that separates
a hand in silhouette
from the bird's pitch.

Over cracks in fake leather,
she lays a wash of white roses. In them, a rainbow
split to wristbands.
You know, the rainbows the kids painted?

Across the table, she narrows her stare,
scorns the lack of words for the waves
that crest and break between us. We don't mention hand,
or eye in back of hand. The tear fallen, the tear about to break.
We don't speak of the skull's eager sockets.

That tree.
That. The only word for it. London Plane
opposite the doctor's surgery, arching its masses
over lines of pavement, road, river. I picture *that tree.*
It sprawls, branches through me – the tree she doesn't paint.

Always a cormorant. Always with its wings spread.

In her small room,
she dots her palette sparingly
with Heavy Body Acrylic.
Brilliant blue for the depths,
left to dry before laying
metallic green, aqua green.

She layers,
blends

until her cormorant eye
looks back

from the London Plane
by Gaol Ferry Bridge.

She steps,
breathes,
harbours,

feels,
doesn't feel
the painting begin.

Super Blood Moon

You rouse me with small sounds:
rifling drawers for lens filters, locking tripod legs.

Through the spare room window:
black river, security light slicking the warehouse roof.

Above the dry dock, Umbra:
moon moving through Earth's inner shadow.

Blind slats are sifting light.
It wavers with the question:

Will I be with you
at the next blood moon?

I know it is wavelengths. I know it is air scattering
blue, allowing only reddish hues

but the dark between us
invites omens.

I am letting knowledge. It flows
from me into the deepening room.

You are squinting into the viewfinder.
I am inviting the ancients.

A jaguar is biting the moon; a sun wolf, giant frog,
severed head of the demon Rahu.

I lay a hand on your back.
Vertebrae press my palm.

I am readying to say rise up,
let's lend our voices to their cries.

The sun and moon are fighting.
Encourage resolution. Let us rest old feuds.

Close windows. Wear something sharp.
Shake your weapons, make the dogs bark.

Elect the proxy. Hide the real king.
The moon is wounded. Cover the food.

Get the pregnant women inside.
Gather the moon wives.

October At Clydey

We watched through glass
from the edge of a pool:
skin steaming, raised from warmth,
cedar walls scenting the room with sap;

our heat, breaths, the water's effusions
settling on French doors,
overlaying Welsh fields
already hazed by storm.

The sky was brushed with storm-light,
but the oak – by day mostly silhouette –
clenched its dark.

All was fluid
beside those branches;
even our limbs,
part-dissolved in blue.

A black that wanted to soak us up.
A black you could sink everything into.

At our backs, the pool:
now settling into fragile stillness,
now twitching.

Crosby

For David Pownall

I

Let's re-start here. Blundellsands.
White lounge of Seaview Guest House.
Emptying pockets of barnacled mussel,
razor clam, limpet, cockle, a curlew feather.
Locked-down months pour from us
as Jack tips sand from a spiral shell.

We read, watch YouTube, learn
what they held, what they were.
Last light a drizzle on black waves,
lives return to feather and shells.

To mussel,
the white foot that peeps,
stretches, probes, drags.
To razor clam, the cream node, burrowing,
until the creature, in its blades of shell,
is lodged in sand.
To mottled feather,
the curlew: oval body
between stilt legs,
curved needle of its bill.

Let's re-start here, on Crosby Beach,
feeling light as the limpet cone
Jack holds between finger and thumb,
index finger of his other hand
scooping out packed sand.

He fills the shell with his memory
of a YouTube clip – points to the lip
as he tells of tentacles,
a toothed tongue scraping algae.

Let's bring to these coils of sand
all we've learnt of lugworm.
We pause over casts,
try to burrow our minds
into wet sand
to flesh
rasping,
sucking,
pistoning water –
ripple of contraction
along bands of muscle
to keep the shaft soft.

I kneel to the scree –
casts left by the sand mason worm
the line thinner this year.

I pick one, raise to your eye
a cylinder of sand, shell fragments
cemented by mucus.

II

To our left, the red dock cranes.
Seaforth windfarm still
while, ahead, on the Burbo flats,
behind a P and O scrawling its wake,
in a blue-tinted haze,
the blades turn.

Over the towers, a vision:
a ferry churning its tracks.
Ahead, the dark haze
of Ireland, Dublin Port,
the day we finally trace ourselves back

to Rampark, Jenkinstown –
my children climbing, called off
the locked gate
between grass slopes,

picking stones from the path
as we gather what we can:

whitewashed cottage
still with red door and window frames
still warding.

At our backs, Rampark Hill:
the pale brown of bare rock
rising from dark greens
the day we finally follow,
wind up
our bloodline.

A man is wading out to swim,
dazzled sea up to his hips.

Time, at last, to hear our own breaths rustle.
Time to notice spray, the sea-seasoning of words
as we speak them.

Wind-snatched, salt-specked, we are stretching
from the tight whorls of lockdown.

On this breadth of sand,
sun-struck shallows,
streaks of black mud,
that daily spiral shrinks
to the turret shell Jack drops on his father's palm.

We paddle runnelling light.
Your foot sucked,
we steer Jack from quicksand.

He buckets a mermaid's purse,
a tooth-white pebble.
Every hope I have for him
rises into my words:
'egg case',
'milky quartz'.

Time, at last, for thoughts to streak
with sun over shallows.
Time to try to explain
the workings of fire,
water,
time:
magma cooling to crystal,
a chip loosed into ocean.
Time to tell
how even gentle waters,
millennia's lightest touch,
will wear the rock smooth.

Near the tideline, I crouch,
pinch black sand,
show Jack the grains.
His eyes lift from specks of magnetite
to breadths of black streaking the beach.

Keep here. Keep to this:
the pebble on my palm, its cold
branching into my blood,
its splash erupting from a rockpool;
Jack's finger denting an air bladder
in a clump of kelp.

He cries out, calls me
to the fine bands of violet
in the shell of the razor clam
he is tilting, raising for me to admire.

III

Poking from the dunes,
two antlers of blanched birch.

Up to his shoulders in dazzle,
the swimmer stretches his arms,
slaps himself. Behind him,
the windfarm turns.

In the arm of my shadow,
a part-buried brick,
corners worn smooth.

They warn that winter may constrict.
We must gather.

Gather
kelped boulders.
Gather
wind rushing marram grass.

Gather
billows of sand
raised by your tread.

Gather
a school of bullheads veering
from shadow to shadow.

Gather runnels –
water alloying with light.

Gather the cargo ship –
its stacked Duplo blocks
we could topple with a finger.

Keepsake
the beached lion's mane jellyfish,
glisters
in the dark ruby of its bell.

Jack charges, shouts at the breakers.
In the pram, our sleeping newborn.
Watch his chest rise and sink.
Listen to breakers of breath.

Gather this patch of beach
twitching with the leaps of sand fleas.

The familiar names will wash back up
but today is Riddle Estuary
Burbo Bank
Blundell Sands
Crosby Beach
Seaview Guest House.

Crucible

Gloucester Cathedral, 2010, 'Crucible' sculpture exhibition

Among the ancient, we almost vanish:
our vague reflections
on Edward II's curled beard.

Someone mumbles "Murder".

The Lady Chapel is tingeing light.
A nude's burnished chest
shows us we are smooth and glorious.

Presbytery. Hirst's flayed martyr
raises a scalpel before the East Window.

Skin draped over his arm,
braided muscles brushed by stained light
slanting through the panes
of nobles, bishops, angels,
his silhouette overlaying hierarchy.

We step onto grass, turn a last time
for the soar of the tower,
follow the path to crescents of box hedge
framing the fountain; to herb beds,
laurel, choisya offering nothing
but their own burgeoning.

We find him in a corner.

Because people watching that day
weren't sure what they saw –
'We thought, at first,
it was all bits of the building' –
Carter fixed the fall,
welded twists of scrap steel.

We don't realise, at first.

We read the plaque:
'Falling Man 9/11, John Sydney Carter.'
Smiles flatten in its sheen.
Gloucester dims – dark mounds
in place of lavender, the rosemary
we rubbed into our fingers.

Someone mutters 'leap of faith'.
A few shadows nod as the rain begins
and everyone but him takes shelter inside.

The Anne Boleyn Fan Club

The boudoir's roped-off, but our bodies still know
the flesh exchange: maid's fingers dabbing heat,
breath into breath,
touch, re-touch,
her eyes moving from the mirror's scrutiny
into chinoiserie's brazen flourish.
We picture her, pent in
by the leer of splayed stamen.

The salon's curves desire us, despite teasels on seats.
French chairs, air taut near the lute.
Any moment, she will resume.

Eileen's read of intrigues
but the caddy drawers are keeping stum.
Secrets hive with specks of tea. She will tremor.
We wait for the bells on the eaves.

They keep the curtains drawn on the long gallery.
Maggie sneers: 'God forbid they're bleached by sun!'
A guide points to pinch of lips, childish hands; lists pigments,
expense. We picture the moted space between her
and mens' translations.

Gold sprouts gold. Candelabras parade.
Thora mispronounces her maiden name.
Gwen tuts. Helen sounds the syllables.

In the grounds, the sun is in the way
though Rose still claims to see the map of her silence.
Near lobelia, excavations: a stab sign
where they picked away for her truths, found trinkets.

The south lawn is littered with picnics.
We eat in the car park, perched on boots,
discuss her between sandwiches,
Marianne's homemade macaroons.

Saturday

For Mum

We were always running for the bus. 56.
Do a reccie, look at the material in Lewis',
George Henry Lees,
finish off in Marks' for Sunday's tea.

You speak of her more, in lockdown – whisk me,
on Facebook Portal, to her brisk Saturdays. 60s Liverpool,
Bootle into town: the Riley girls, pushing the baby.
We were always running for the bus. 56.

I watch walls, the cast of light. A year since
the decorator sanded, layered cream.
I am stranded on plains of 'slipper satin'.
Do a recce, look at the material in Lewis'.

Ants cross the garden table.
Pink rose going over. I pinch off hips, brown heads;
cut back hostas, laid waste by tiny snails.
George Henry Lees.

Spring contracted to nextdoor's maple,
I check the borders for crowns, seek the company
of returning perennials
finish off in Marks' for Sunday's tea.

Braids

After climbing Yat Rock
after kayaks cut tracks through The Wye
after helming the might of a piebald mare
along paths walled in hawthorn
breaks gifting brief, airy brinks
glimpses of the Severn
I braided her hair
I braided in the high air
I caught the peregrine's keen
drew it through the weave

With hands that braved cliff spiders
the brush of white egg sacks
precious, precarious pendants
With hands that braved the mothers
scurrying from their nooks
satin beads of their bodies
twitching on limestone lips
I braided her hair
I braided in the silk
soft as fog round their young
I braided in that strength
I braided in the high air
I caught the peregrine's keen
drew it through the weave

My body told its secrets that day
a grip in my fingertips
I could hang my whole weight on
Under the lash of wind
I was tensile as guy-lines
latched tight as toadflax
florets of fleabane
I braided in that strength
I braided in the high air
I caught the peregrine's keen
drew it through the weave

With hands that pulsed a river
oars sweeping light
as rain quickened the Wye
I braided her hair
I gathered the foam
wreathing boulders in New Weir Rapids
I gathered echoes
our calls returned larger, clearer
by an iron arch of Town Bridge
I gathered the blurring banks
I gathered willow, alder
I gathered beech and ash
I braided in that strength
I braided in the high air
I caught the peregrine's keen
drew it through the weave

With hands that steered a willful pony
with a tug, flick of an ankle
I braided her hair
I braided in the shades
fleeting through its mane
I braided in that strength
I braided in the high air
I caught the peregrine's keen
drew it through the weave

In our hotel room
I braided in the night
We pushed our beds together
bridged our secrets
I promised to always be there
to untangle her, even in the dark
I braided in that strength
I braided in the high air
I caught the peregrine's keen
drew it through the weave

Dart

For Chris Thomas

We used to walk past one on our way to college.
Everything else was green
and then this great black bird — oily black —
always on the same rock, always its wings outspread,
like it grew from shadow.

You stop on the bank
between town and the art college you hate;
portfolio propped against your leg,
less time around your eyes.

We called it The Devil Bird.

Bucket hat, Pokémon watch,
pack of fags in your anorak,
thinner frames on your spectacles
(the black, retro frames came later).

'Did you see it?' we'd ask. It was like nothing else:
everything was green. Small birds.

Who is there now?
A student? Do they sense you
beside them on the bank?
The Dart, its oaks and willows;
another spectral, storied bird
on the rock.

You are straying from me;
from Ercol tables, nouveau posters,
your chipped mug of black, sugary tea.

You return to waterwheel,
the walls of a barn —
to eddies and rock
to cormorant.

Cousin

For Stuart

In the car park, shouldering Christmas trees. Cannop Valley holds you.
Smiling, feigning annoyance: 'We've been non-stop!' Cannop Valley holds you.
Behind you, Dean slopes – tiers of spruce, fir, birch, oak, larch.
Cannop Valley holds you.
In the kitchen, slicing mum's homegrown cucumbers, tomatoes for the do.
Cannop Valley holds you.
Bathroom you painted blue. 'It looks good, doesn't it!'
Cannop Valley holds you.
Shed door you painted blue.
Cannop Valley holds you.
That time, by the yard gate, we praised mum's chili jam. 'I've got a jar to take home.'
Cannop Valley holds you.
That time, in the lounge, you watched my Jack. 'I can see nan.'
Cannop Valley holds you.
Thick white bread ham sandwiches. Mum: 'He doesn't eat,
then he comes here and eats like a horse.' Cannop Valley holds you.
Black coffee. Three heaped spoons. Cannop Valley holds you.
I was learning how to win that deep-lined smile. Cannop Valley holds you.

'No doctors. Quacks!' Cannop Valley keeps you.
Your teenage daughter: 'He didn't want to be old bones.' Cannop Valley keeps you.
Motorbike helmet still hung in the shed. Cannop Valley keeps you.
Screws still tight on the wheels of Jack's walker. Cannop Valley keeps you.
Faintest impression of you by the new patio
where the yard gate used to be. Cannop Valley keeps you.
Faintest impression outside the shop door. Mirage in the car park.
Cannop Valley keeps you.

Statues

Pygmy Pinetum Garden Nurseries, July 2020

Among the statues –
first visit since lockdown –
my son dips his finger in a bird bath.
Limestone cockle on a plinth.

I watch it refracted,
want to snatch his hand back
from the algae-slimed dreg of rain
cupping, altering
sky,
silver birch,
my child;
reminding me
he will be changed.

He wipes his hand on his shorts,
returns to me
telling of the tricks of water.

Shadows quiver
on a replica Easter Island Head.

He will be changed.

For now, just this: small hands
gesturing wonder;
yellow hair, red coat;

momentary angling
of light waves.

Their Cormorants

Robbie's Cormorant
Almost my first ever poem was on the cormorant.
One I met underwater whilst diving.

Lucy's Cormorant
After her partner's interview,
after the panic attack,
lost glasses,
late train,
heat,
ginger beer and Mena Dhu at the Mill on the Exe.
We watched a cormorant spread its wings
as though alone in holding the weight of the day;
its wingspan tip to tip a portent
for the end of one chapter, the beginning of another.

Fiona's Cormorant
I swim or snorkel all year round
and see them at my local beach.
They pose on rocks, fish, dry their wings.
I think the ones there at the moment
are actually Mediterranean shags
but I am calling them cormorants
to stop the naff jokes.
Lovely green eyes
if you see them up close.
If one dives under you while you're snorkelling,
it is a bit frightening
because of the speed at which they move.

Julia's Cormorant
Stretching their wings
in the early mornings
while I stand-up paddleboard
on Bristol harbour.

Laura's Cormorant
We used to see them out of my window
when I lived in Redcliffe.

Paul's Cormorant
Fair Isle, Sutherland,
their necks shimmering
above rocks flayed by sea.

John's Cormorant
It seemed puzzled, like me
when I came to Bristol during the war.
Blitzed city. Young man finding
something grand, something gilded
among the ruins.

Clare's Cormorant
He had just tried to leave her.
I mean all I want is for things to go back to how they were before.
I mean, I'm not being funny, it wasn't perfect, don't get me wrong.
Between yachts, outside The Watershed.
What is that? Where's it gone?
Leaving his 'I don't love you',
weeks of fights and silence,
to follow its breath.
Look! You can see where it is from the bubbles.
I never even knew we had birds like that.

Dad's Cormorant
On the canals, we watched anglers throw bricks at them.
Like a rite of passage: if you were an angler,
you had to hate cormorants.

Octopus

For Nanny Riley

Her first is stillborn,
but the doctor leans in with an order:
'Don't cry. You'll have a baker's dozen.'

Now thirteen reach into her sleep.

She tucks them into bunkbeds,
the baby in the rattan crib,
only to find them seeking her
where she is nooked
in the reef of sleep.

A dream of octopus legs:
body unseen,
just arms probing the dark
to claim her, to select
which part of her to suck.

Waking with the trace of it
wriggling on the ceiling,
his wheezy snore beside her,
she checks her arms, legs,
peeps into the neck of her nightie,
half-expecting welts.

Only when ten children have moved out,
only when there is space –
a room for each,
beds to spare;

only when the giant
from books and pictures
with a ship in its clutch
is deflated to truth:

a soft bulb trailing
eight undulating,
sensuous arms;

only then does she tell
how her children
once muscled and squeezed
into her nights.

Dear Leonardo,

Couldn't stay long, had to lift him up to meet you,
thought he might squirm, but your lines caught him
long enough for a lady in a gauzy scarf
to say 'Ah, lovely' at his gaze, as he followed sinews.
She looked longer at him than at the massy vines
of the bronchi, intricate hearts chiaroscuro under dim lamps,
a cow's uterus, wombs neat as nutshells, Christ with a lamb,
a bear's foot, horse's anus, mortars, crossbows, projectiles.

She will return to this: your anatomies, the child's curls
shining on his temples, his every nerve, every fibre
wandering your lines, asking with more than words.
A golden ratio, the web spun between you
nothing could break; his eyes on a hunched foetus:
sepia bud, all lines furled.

Chick

Years, the lone bird on the crooked stick,
now with partner and chick
high in a willow
above the northern lake.

Slight shift. Of bird, of light.
We catch sight of the chick's silver-white chest.

> My father
> in The Tower.
> Brown storey on brown storey
> over the car park.
> Row of lift doors. Ward C.
> High metal bed. Plastic curtain.
> Shared sink in the corner.

The Tower is here, over willow;
over the ripple-scudding mallard.
It is here
but barely heeded, today –
our eyes busied with leaves
that flash as we rise
through willow
to three cormorants;
to renewal,
silver-white.

On the causeway,
between reeds, club rush of Cannop marsh
and the lake mirroring oaks,
yesterday's conversation

> *I thought I had donkeys' years with him.*
> *Well, the sort of man he was,*
> *how he's always been so well.*
> *This was never going to happen.*

is gusted from my clutch,
strewn through the bough of an oak

that has laid its shadow on the water
for the 33 years we have walked here.

On the jetty, a vow:
to yellow streak of gular pouch,
to silver white chest,

to my father, in The Tower,
I vow I will rush,
I will flare.

Stop on the bridge
where marsh water
slides into lake.

> *I've known for years*
> *this would happen to your dad.*

Mum's words fall from me
as the reeds we dropped in Poohsticks.
I watch her words glide shallow water
out, into lake, to pike, carp;
to the centre,
water slicking into the round gape
of the shaft spillway.

In the lit greens of the wooded bank,
between trunks, we glimpse lake and light,
look for the cormorants' tree.

> *Hilary said I can't believe*
> *this has happened to Keith.*

Hilary's shock, our shock ever-renewing
swept up into alder, silver birch.

Clare points to a white trunk.

In leaf and light,
a nuthatch
drops down a branch.

I swear they were in a willow
with a crook in its trunk.

Back across, we spy them again.
Beneath three crows,
a glance of silver-white chest;
parents a branch below,
wings stretched to dry.

Clare's sighing smile:
'Lizzie, you were close.
If we'd just looked to the right.'

The crows drop to pester
but the family holds fast.

The Latch

On the phone in lockdown,
mum tells me about nan:
I remember her watching me latch Clare on.
She'd be on tenterhooks,
wincing because I was so sore.
She was desperate for me to breastfeed.

First feed of the day,
hand cupping his head,
crescent pillow round my waist,
I carried him, sleeping, to the garden,
her voice tucked
between shoulder and chin.

My gaze trailing Little Rambler
to pink ruffs, orange hips,
bees,
I breathed more easily,
felt enclosed
in a stronghold of mothers,

latched him on
as a bee dipped for nectar.

Through it all,
the milk.

Through it all,
the call,
the flow,
the flutter,
the suck.

Stonehenge

I had expected touch, not cordons,
barely glanced at the monoliths,
returned to rippling grass,
the steward with a rook on her hand.

I barely glanced at the monoliths
refaced by shadow.
The rook crammed his cheeks with seeds,
jackdaws peeled lichen from the sarsens.

Shadows refaced the stones.
Need sharpened,
plucked sheep's fleece from barbs,
padded nests in the lintels.

Need sharpened: its curved tip
snagged strength from woods,
braced nests in the lintels.
I understood parents building forts from scraps,

pilfering softness, the forest's strength.
Sentry crows scouted from fence posts.
I understood parents building forts from scraps.
I understood roosts, hunger, hands casting seeds.

Sentry crows scouted from fence posts,
pecked carrion, mobbed a carcass near the Altar Stone.
I understood hunger, bones picked clean, hands casting seeds.
I didn't quiver. Ley lines failed to pluck my blood.

I understood crows mobbing carrion:
a coven feasting near the Altar Stone.
I didn't quiver. No tug of ley lines on my blood
only the rustle of a paper bag, rush of seeds.

The coven lifted, black flurry scattering
as the sun flung a final lance.
Paper rustled, seeds rushed onto palm,
hills moulted colour, night closed its seal.

The Lye

For my Chris
Bristol, April 2020 (first national lockdown)

You come to me in the lounge
– say *It could be a poem. Come outside.* –
smiling wide as the garden, vivid
as the green tomatoes, white strawberries
our son pinches off and presents.

I found it by the outdoor tap. The lye.
I thought it could be a poem. It won't wash off.
Like the lies… As far as you'll go.

I touch above the tap,
stroke red bricks waxy smooth,
try to pick with a nail

the months latching the alley gate,
lathering on the Savon de Marseilles
we bought back from Normandy –

slipping it from the cellophaned multipack,
fingertips tracing the carved name –

used now to a nub; blanked,
fissured with grime,
your banker's hands chapped for the first time.

Look at this.
You'd held out an open hand:
skin cracked on palms,
tops of fingers.

Wash after diligent wash
spattering the wall
petrifying.

The Spell

After she left, I rifled her plot,
found my cure thriving, lengthening its stems
through the life she left behind.

Her own soil has nourished the nine
that will purge me of her.

She never read, never knew The Lacnunga.
I draw its roots, obey its verbs,
bow my voice to each quiver of herbs.

To lamb's cress, I singe – Stune that grew on stone.
To mayweed, its white coronet, I singe.
I singe to its soft yellow eyes.

To waybread of the roadsides, I singe – mother of herbs,
withstanding the loads of bulls and brides.
I singe to nettle that expels malignant things.

To fennel, I singe – that avails against three and against thirty.
I singe to chamomile, to a fistful of chervil.

With peppermint breaths, I singe.
I singe aniseed. I singe notes laced with liquorice.

With scented fingers, I singe.
I singe to spikelets of cockspur.
With grimed fingernails, I rake off its bristled seeds.

To mugwort, I singe – Una, oldest of herbs.
Because she is attre, geblaed, wyrm,

I wyrc slypan of wætere and of axsan.
I genim finol, wyl on þære slyppan.

Pestling petals, roots, stems, I singe.
While I grind the brittle, the silks, I singe.

To a sweet grease, I singe.
I singe as I salve myself with the sticky gleam.

I singe with myself, while the charm swells on the glass.
Three times, as it shrinks and clings, I singe:
over mirrored mouth, each ear, my chest.

With the woman in the mirror, I singe.
I singe with the unrequited.
I singe as Redcliffe tolls the hour
with its cast iron tongue.

I singe with a millennium of vengeance
warming my lips.

I Choose River

Tonight I choose river
not the new laid road, but the bank –
to fall in step
with the eights plying black water
clunk in oarlock, whip through air.

I meet the coxswain's dare,
fall in step with flux of muscle,
clunk in oarlock, whip through air.

Tonight I choose river
not to let the dark cling
but to lever it,
lift free,
leave it quivering.

I choose ancient slipstreams
not bars, restaurants,
neon's pulsing hunger
but wherrymen
raising quicksilver ripples.

Overlord with Declan

At Arromanches, the Channel rushes,
breaks against concrete caissons,
the dark, gapped line of Mulberry B, a mile from Declan
dipping small hands, stirring up gobies.

He strokes the pearl inlay of an upturned fiddler crab,
gifts it to me – a stoop font, offering a slip of sky.

Declan has memorised the history.
Water flashes on his arm as he prods the horizon,
his finger stubbing out a yacht.

He tells of Iorys Hughes, 1942, sketching plans:
his pencil towing fine lines, ruling steel roads,
lightly shading six thousand tonne caissons.
The white space on the page is choppy today.
It lurches, claims.

Declan plucks a mermaid's purse,
pinches the empty egg case.
Shallows simper to our toes
as he describes the mock-up:
paper boats floated in a bathtub on the Queen Mary.
He deepens his voice for Mountbatten:
'More waves please, Lieutenant Grant.'

There is a dazzle on Declan's lower lip
as he tells of a bath brush
urging a ripple through the tub,
the paper fleet keeping afloat
in the ring of a Mae West lifebelt.

He pincers a trawler between index and thumb,
cuts to two years later:
Hughes' design translated
to tonnes of concrete, steel,
scuttled merchant ships
hefted by tugs across the Channel.

We wade to our knees.
Water rears, displays its weed
as Declan raises his index finger,
draws lost lines on air.
Pierheads, steel roadways
fanning toward the shore.

A child's finger to blot out a caisson,
one hand to hide the whole.

Come To The Bottom Of His Garden

Leave his top lawn. Here it's wilder:
just a few stones, a slope, a step
to reach the sound of water.
He will never say what you need.

Just a few stones, a slope, a step.
Join me at the white-barked walnut tree.
He will never say what you need.
Lean on a fencepost. Breathe the woods below.

Join me at the white-barked walnut tree.
You have waited too long for his praise.
Lean on a fencepost. Breathe the woods below.
Watch magpies dip into aisles of fir.

You have waited too long for his praise.
Let stickyweed lay its claim.
Watch magpies dip into aisles of fir.
Sit with me in clover.

That River

I've been watching,
reading too much bad news.
10pm, a metaphor:
I am that river.
Citarum. Rubbish dump.

The photo online.
One small boat
figure in white jumper, black shoulder bag
squatting in the prow
his wake
the only water visible –
a fragment of light and reflection
beneath the bow

a gasp
sealed up moments later
by trash.

I scrapped the metaphor
but the photograph –
rubbish dump dotted
with clumps of water hyacinth

his wake

that small, gleaming break
in the crap –

I pass that
to you.

The Eighth Fish

Every household keeps cormorants.
There is fish with every meal – Li Shizen, *Bencao Gangmu*

What is the eighth fish to you?
Why have you walked Bristol streets
thinking of the fisherman
who plies oars through lotus,
lily beds on Lake Baiyangdian,
his boat crewed by cormorants
perched on crooked sticks
along the sides?
Why, on Dean Street, on Vauxhall Bridge,
do you keep thinking of the bird,
its tally achieved,
waiting, after the seventh eel
or thrashing hulk of carp,
for its pittance: the eighth fish, a tiddler,
flung to its yawning hunger.

The Yangtze, the Mekong:
what are these great rivers to you?
Li, Huai, Huang He:
what business have they here,
in your mind all day
while you navigate this narrow city?
String tied loosely around the throat,
its instinct constricted.
A brief struggle, a question
darting across its ancient eye,
ancestral reptile rising, then subdued,
the bird surrendering to the present,
the fisherman's chant,
his dance rocking the boat
until his fish hawk launches,
fires into deep water,
follows the dark flight paths
of his need.

Pole dipped, bird secured,
lifted on its pivot, landed,
its gullet swelling behind the string
with a fish it can't swallow.
Why are you fixated on this?
Fledgling trained
until its master's voice is a leash.
One thousand three hundred years
of his weathered hands
massaging the serpentine neck
for the prize: catfish, ayu
delivered in a triumph of obedience.

In the flare of an August afternoon,
why do you picture the blue hour?
Master squatting opposite his heedful cormorant,
lantern between them,
their task illumined,
the question illumined:
how much writhing silver
will they eke from the night?

The Doll Hospital

For Mum and Nanny Riley

No arms. The clothes in a state. We'd pull out the hair.
Eyes poked in or fallen out. Hollow heads.
You couldn't hook the limbs back on.
Hard plastic, not porcelain – not that old.

Anything that couldn't be repaired
was thrown out. There was no space.
She wouldn't have them in the house like that.

She always left it late.
December. Running for the 56.
She'd take one or two of us.
The eldest, usually.

St John's Gardens.
I remember it was near the bus station.
Brownlow Hill. The Doll Hospital.
Never been in a building that tall.

The stairs. Bare wood.
All our houses were modern. Carpeted.
These were little. Rickety.
Right up to the top floor

with a big bag full of dolls.
I'd never climbed that many
never been in a building that old.
Small, crowded; things up the walls,
glass-fronted cabinets, shelves full of dolls.

Each Christmas, we got them back
beautifully dressed. Wigged. Fresh stuffing.
Arms and legs re-attached.

She made their clothes from off-cuts
of our new summer frocks
curtains, cot frills from the rest.

The last time we went,
it was evening, pouring with rain.

She always left it late.
We'd have been rushing to collect.

Edie

After words
you hope there is no more to her
than blended monochromes, glossed lip.
But that sidelong look?
You are regretting your flippancy.

Edie has kept it all:
blue Steepletone,
bowl of purple croci,
his backward glance
from the porch of the painted wagon;

gold-banded antique globe,
Hotpoint fridge, always full
(stacked Tupperware, ham on the bone,
scarlet cathedral of the gummy-moulded jelly).

A nook of Edie
is still crammed with the summer
they crashed the red Chevrolet.
His silhouette
too close to the edge.

Edie is not afraid of revelation.
Spittlebug unclasping wings
from a striped thorax;
moth orchid's lascivious gape.

Edie has cut a slice from Earth,
keeps in mind
its concentric heats.

Edie is dwelling on your throwaway words.

You are looking back at that face,
that look.

Edie is collaging her connotations.

Seated Spirit of Justice,
her arms raised, pointing;
her counterpart's dropped shoulders,
his open palms.

Mournful gaze of orangutang.

Coral
Camelia
Lily
Cyclamen
Ostrich fern
Shelf fungus.

Eye-lined, sheened lip; high, smooth cheek.
That look has you asking
what sprang, only now to land?
What launched, only now to roost?
What seeded, only now to root?

It is Edie's American robin   her owl   It is Edie's hawk moth

                                                                 her sloth

                              her toucan   It is Edie's helicopter
                                           her three-masted ship
                        It is her wolfhound
                                  her grey parrot

                    It is Edie's tiger

                                                    her cheetah
her streamertail hummingbird.

You wish you had been more careful.

Sonnets Of Separation

I

We were already between worlds. Dementia.
That word pervading the week Cannop Brook breached,
fogged water claiming our wood. 'It's leached',
Dad said, 'from the coal seam. There's grey clay.'
We looked for brown trout, bellying sandbars,
shifting between light and shade,
moments settling, only to be shattered
by the brook's relentless replenishment.

I asked: 'How you doing, Dad?'
'Oh, you know, chasing thin air.'
Already a borderland. Mum joking:
'We've got Lewy bodies dancing round the room,
getting blamed for everything.'
You, in me, stirring against another threshold.

II

You, in me, stirring against another threshold,
soon to break into our days' tight circuit:
muted street, empty car park, the cradles
of our cracked, anti-bac'd hands. No parade,

no displaying you in North Street cafes,
no strangers laying praise on your new skin.
Adoration of grandparents, uncles, aunts
cordoned from two-metre sanctuaries.

My warning glare, willing air to defend us –
willing Sue, bringing smiles, best wishes too near;
Bob, approaching the front wall of his drive
with a joke about leper colonies,

to feel the hard border of my fear. Your cries reel
across crowdless stadium, parked-up street.

III

Your cries reel across crowdless stadium, parked-up street.
Grandparents digital. Forest of Dean faltering
on screen. Your Nana hoping spring, summer's flow will reach,
hovering her phone over their garden centre.
Behind the 'Closed' sign, peonies unwrap themselves,
salvia's blue profusions, lily of the valley,
silver-edged iris sibirica, azaleas

split to pixels by a brittle Wi-Fi signal.
Season of stammered translations.
Internet traffic. Marooned bodies
reaching with radiowaves, a surge of longing

interrupting symphonies of green, curving paths,
glide of stem to sepal, the brook's relentless rush.

IV

Glide of stem to sepal, the brook's relentless rush;
we will wade again, chew a wild mint leaf, watch for trout
in the stirred sand, lift echinacea, eryngium
for their cupped dusk. There will be tides of touch

when we breach these lockdown dams: two metres,
twenty motorway miles, the white, buffeted bridge
to your grandad, finally holding you.

The Watchers

Of something far more deeply interfused,
Whose dwelling is the light of setting suns,
And the round ocean and the living air,
And the blue sky, and in the mind of man.
  — William Wordsworth, *Tintern Abbey.*

I

They watch day shrink to a line
in always too much sky.
Rusted eyes sweep for news
know there is no use searching light
or the sea's dark knots; no use
fathoming for truth among the wavering shoots
of something far more deeply interfused.

II

Gull keens, a frigate's low horn,
light stippling sleek water
while tides change in their rusted minds.
A surge in the blood, vision of the lost ship
whose dwelling is the light of setting suns.

III

They have watched so long
time has mapped them with frail rinds
and oxide blisters.
Every day their grief brightens
as they let themselves rust,

the bodies' changing tides laid bare
as they hold the water's gaze,
sift along the streak of last light
and the round ocean and the living air.

IV

They watch the beach forget.
Their lost survive in corroding chests,
eyes so brittle they have begun to flake.
They trail the breeze through cupped hands
but there is no sign in the cycles that graze them,
no hint in bristling marram, the deep suck of sand.

On the horizon, final fusion of sea and sun
snuffed, leaves their fissured stares, their blazing rusts.
No hope in blinking cities, swathes of farmland
and the blue sky, and in the mind of man.

Celia In The Garden

Celia and I stand apart in the garden.
Behind her, dahlias' symmetric rays,
salvia and thyme bristling with hoverflies;
African Queen's splitting buds,
its single blown flame;
You Are Beautiful
bowed by the weight
of its abundance.

Celia looks away. I follow her gaze –
dark brown, steady,
framed in the black strokes of her cat's eye liner –
to a bee tucking itself into a foxglove
its silhouette shifting in the cup.
Between us, a look.
There is too much.
Lockdown words hover. *Strange. Weird. Bizarre.*
I snatch them, crush them in my fist.
Between us, the scented air spores and swarms.

In the cool of the kitchen,
her quiet voice
as I spoon coffee:
'I've had three miscarriages.'

★

Third summer she's kept away.
By purple phlox, tiger lily in bud,
an after-image:
her set mouth, narrowed eyes
defying blue asters,
pink penstemon,
the lavish sun.

The salvia is late to flower.
I've no idea what's happened to the foxglove.

No-one on the picnic site.
Shuttered coffee hut.
Quiet of the northern lake
pipped by the calls of coots
ripped by the hilarity of mallards
re-sealing over the slow steps
of the lone cormorant
hopping onto the jetty
splatting one black foot
in front of the other.

Notes

In 'You Began', the Slighe Chualann is an ancient roadway which stretched from the residence of the High King of Ireland at Tara to the lands of Cuala. Cu Cuchulain is an Irish mythological hero who appears in the stories of the Ulster Cycle. Sin-sin-seanmháthair is Irish for great-great grandmother, and sin-seanathair for great-grandfather.

'The Spell' refers to the 'Nine Herbs Charm', a remedy in *The Lacnunga* – a tenth century collection of Anglo-Saxon medical texts and prayers, written in Old English and Latin. The poem contains several of the Old English names for the nine herbs, as well as excerpts of descriptions, slightly re-worded.

> *attre, geblaed, wyrm*: poison, blister, serpent.
> *I genim finol, wil on þære slyppan*: make a paste of water
> and of ash; take the fennel, boil in the paste.

Redcliffe refers to St Mary Redcliffe Church, Bristol.

'Edie' was written after the artwork *Edie* by Maria Rivans, the cover image of my first collection *In Her Shambles*.

In 'Sonnets of Separation', Lewy bodies are abnormal aggregations of protein that develop inside nerve cells, contributing to Parkinson's disease (PD), the Lewy body dementias (Parkinson's disease dementia and dementia with Lewy bodies), and some other disorders.

'The Watchers' was inspired by the sculpture *Another Place* by Antony Gormley, located at Crosby Beach, Liverpool.

Acknowledgements

I am grateful to the following journals, in which some of these poems have appeared: 'Cormorant' in *Poetry Salzburg Review* (Issue 38); 'Overlord With Declan' and 'The Watchers' in the anthology *Time And Tide* (Arachne Press, 2019); 'Sonnets Of Separation' in online anthology *Write Where We Are Now* (Carol Ann Duffy and Manchester Writing School at MMU, 2020); 'October at Clydey', 'Octopus', 'Edie' in *Raceme* (Issue 13); 'Coulouvray', 'Dart' in *Tears In The Fence* (Issue 78).

I would like to thank writer David Pownall and his family. Novelist, playwright, poet, David died in November, 2022. Dear David, we didn't know each other for long, but I feel so fortunate to have read with you at two very special events and to have chatted with you over email, at events and at your beautiful home. Our short talks and your wonderful books and plays will continue to influence and inspire me. Thank you.

I would like to thank my fellow members of poetry quartet The Spoke for their guidance and support. I would also like to thank wonderful poet Julie-ann Rowell, who has been an invaluable mentor.

I would like to thank my family, who inspired many of the poems. Thank you to Marie for her words in 'Paddy's Ashes' and to my mother for her words in 'Saturday' and 'The Doll Hospital'.

Thank you to Farah, Josie, Nick, Martina, Immy and Elicia for providing an inspiring, atmospheric space for creativity, as well as gorgeous coffee, toasties and cakes in lovely Farahway Cafe! Many of the poems in this collection were drafted and honed there. Thank you to Farah and Josie for comforting me when I found losing my brilliant father to dementia overwhelming and to Nick for his kindness when my sister died.

Thank you to Nook Café for delicious coffee and a great space in which to write. Thank you to Isobel in particular for her kind words as I grieve for my sister.

Thank you to my dear, supremely talented friends, artists Gemma Compton and Chris Thomas, who inspired the poems 'Dart', '10,000 Steps' and 'Celia In The Garden'. Thank you to Gemma for letting us use her glorious painting '10,000 Steps' as the book cover.